START

Origami

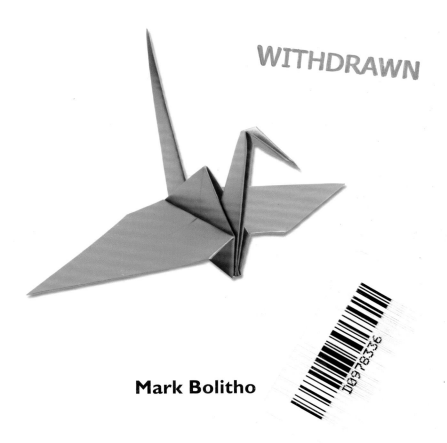

Mark Bolitho

START

Origami

All the techniques and tips you need to get you started

Mark Bolitho

Search Press

This edition published in Great Britain in 2012 by
Search Press Limited
Wellwood, North Farm Road
Tunbridge Wells, Kent TN2 3DR

Copyright © 2012 Axis Books Ltd

Created and conceived by
Axis Books Ltd
8c Accommodation Road
London NW11 8ED
www.axispublishing.co.uk

Creative Director: Siân Keogh
Editor: Anna Southgate
Design: Marie Christou
Production: Bili Books

ISBN 978-1-84448-738-7

The Publishers and author can accept no responsibility for any
consequences arising from the information, advice or instructions given in
this publication. Readers are permitted to reproduce any of the origami
in this book for their personal use, or for the purposes of selling for
charity, free of charge and without the prior permission of the Publishers.
Any use of the items for commercial purposes is not permitted
without the prior permission of the Publishers.

Suppliers
If you have difficulty in obtaining any of the materials and
equipment mentioned in this book, please visit the Search Press website
for details of suppliers: www.searchpress.com
Alternatively, you can write to the Publishers at the address above,
for a current list of stockists, which includes firms
who operate a mail-order service.

Printed in China

Contents

Introduction

Origami is the art of folding paper. It is a practice that has emerged over time, from traditional designs passed between generations to sophisticated complex designs that have been invented in the last fifty years. There are no strict rules in paper folding. However, there is a school of thought that advocates a classic origami style requiring a model to be made from an uncut square.

Origami is the Japanese word for paper folding and the art is associated with Japanese culture. The name was adopted by origami societies outside Japan in the 1950s and it soon became the international name for the art of folding paper.

The earliest records of folded design are Japanese and some now called traditional models can be seen in early wood cuts and prints. These early models involved a few folds, but complex design was limited by the technical quality and size of paper that was manufactured at the time. Paper was also a more expensive commodity and not as widely available as it is today.

Moving away from its traditional roots, modern origami can be classified into various genres. Naturalistic or lifelike origami is the re-creation of animals, birds and objects. These designs attempt to capture the essence of an object in a folded form. Geometric origami has a more mathematical basis. It is possible to make different shapes from either a single sheet of paper or using many modules that weave together. Another area that has evolved is origami tessellation where a sheet is folded to create a patterned surface.

Many of the models presented in this collection are mathematical in their design. The folding process will often rely on mathematical principles as the folds evolve such as dividing the paper in parts or folding an edge to a particular point. Some origami designs can be used to explain and demonstrate mathematical principles and it is increasingly being used as an educational tool in the classroom. In recent years a more complex mathematics of origami has been developed. The tools that have evolved from this can be used in origami design to produce crease patterns that can be folded to a particular design (the crease pattern shows the creases that need to be folded to construct a particular model). Mathematical theory and crease patterns are more advanced origami techniques. You do not have to have any mathematical knowledge to follow origami instructions.

This book is an introduction to paper folding. It is organised into five sections. The first section, Basic folds, introduces the fundamental concepts of origami and the process of following instructions. All of the models in this section are made using very simple folds. By following these exercises, you will become familiar with the step-by-step diagrams that are often used to explain a folding process. The Basic techniques section gradually introduces more advanced folding techniques and different types of folds along with folded examples of models that use the technique being explored. The third section, All

shapes and sizes, presents some origami designs that are made from shapes other than squares. The fourth section, Modular origami, introduces a style of origami that uses more than one sheet of paper in its construction. The final section, Advanced projects, presents some more complex models for you to experiment with.

With origami almost anything is possible. This book presents a collection of designs with a gradual increase in complexity. It shows how subjects can be presented within the limitations of a folded square of paper. Hopefully it will inspire you to further creativity through your choice of paper to execute the models. Try experimenting by modifying the models presented or creating your own designs.

The satisfaction of origami comes not only from creating interesting designs but also from following the folding journey and seeing your model evolve at your fingertips.

A brief history of origami

Paper was invented in China in the first century AD and it is assumed that inevitably paper folding probably began at the same time. This may not be the case as early paper may not have had the same properties of paper as we know it today. The Egyptians had used papyrus but its composition meant that it was not malleable enough to bend without breaking. Surviving written documents from this period are generally rolled into scrolls, rather than folded.

By the eighth century paper had reached Japan. Historical records from the period feature some evidence of folded designs such as the O-Shide or Gohei, a zigzag folded paper used in Shinto shrines. Later records show structured paper wrappers being used for gifts, sometimes referred to as Noshi. Many of the early Japanese models were ceremonial folds that were passed down through generations.

The first printed record is thought to be a book of Japanese woodcut designs called the 'Ranma Zushiki'. It was printed in 1734 and features a

woodcut design composed of sophisticated origami images, including the traditional crane, four legged box, a boat and a hooded monk. The first known book of origami instructions was published in 1797. 'Senbazaru Orikata' or 'The Secrets of One Thousand Cranes Origami' included instructions based on the traditional crane design. The book features a fold pattern for the crane model along with template patterns showing where to cut the paper to prepare the multiple crane models.

Trade brought paper to Europe. By the fourteenth century paper was being manufactured in the West. This inevitably lead to practical paper folding required for storing or transporting larger sheets and paper products such as maps. As paper manufacturing technology developed, paper as a product became more similar to paper as we know it today. Paper that was thinner and more malleable began to emerge.

A European paper folding tradition probably arose simultaneously to the introduction of paper manufacturing. One of the earliest known European designs is Spanish. Called the 'Parajita', it is a bird like model. The earliest known surviving folded European model is a model of a horse and rider dating from 1810 and held in a collection at the German National Museum at Nuremburg. In the nineteenth century as the Japanese cultural influence began to grow, there is evidence of origami being demonstrated in Europe by travelling magicians who had learned their craft in

Japan. It is thought that the traditional flapping bird was introduced to a European audience through this method. Stage magicians were also adopting origami into their routines. The famed escapologist Harry Houdini published a book entitled 'Paper Magic'.

By the 1960s an international diagramming style had emerged following correspondence between the Japanese, Akira Yoshizawa and the American, Samuel Randlett. Their terminology was adopted by the origami community and meant that origami ideas and designs could be exchanged internationally.

Although origami has an ancient heritage, most of the evolution of the art has taken place in recent times. This has been due to the exchange of ideas between enthusiasts as well as the emergence of paper technology and different manufacturing processes that enable more

compex models to be designed and realised. Some designers manufacture their own paper to present the forms they have created to best effect.

Origami societies have emerged outside Japan and active groups exist in countries including Britain, France, Germany, the Netherlands and USA. Many of these groups host international conventions of their members on a regular basis and enthusiasts from all over the world meet up and exchange their ideas and enthusiasm.

Modern origami has evolved as a fusion of Eastern and Western influences. In Japan a new generation of origami enthusiasts has emerged and in turn innovative designs from Western folders have been taken back to Japan. New styles of folding are emerging such as modular constructions, origami tessellation patterns, wet folding and crumpling which create more abstract fold patterns and designs.

Paper

All paper can be folded, but choosing the right paper to create your origami models can make a huge difference to the finished piece. If the paper is too thick it can tear when folded, too elastic and it will not hold the creases.

As origami is all about folding paper, the choice of paper is an important part of the process. All paper can be folded. However, paper composition can affect its ability to hold a crease which impacts its suitability to be used to create folded models. A paper's suitability depends on the quality and thickness of the paper used. If paper is too thick it may break when a fold is applied as the fibres are strained in the process. If the paper has a greater elasticity it may not be able to hold a crease when folded. Paper manufacture is a technical process. When paper is produced it is classified by its weight. This is a specification called gsm, or 'grams per square metre'. This specification gives a weight of a square metre of the paper. This is an important consideration as the higher the weight, or gsm, the thicker the paper will be. For folded paper projects generally the thinner the paper the better. However, for larger projects it may be worth investigating papers with a higher weight as it may enhance the structure of the final model.

The most suitable paper is a lightweight paper with a high malleability that will hold a crease when folded. Choice of colour is also important from a design perspective and should be a consideration before embarking on a project. Lighter colours will show off creases better and natural colours will create a more organic feel to the final model. Patterned papers can be particularly effective and you can create beautiful designs using Japanese washi paper.

Specific origami paper can be purchased. It is generally available in 15 cm squares, and is readily available in a wide variety of colours and patterns. Its weight is about 70 gsm. However, if you cannot obtain origami paper, paper of a weight up to 100 gsm is just as suitable for most origami projects.

Equipment

You can do origami using just your hands. However there are some things that will make folding and shaping paper a lot easier and they will also help you to create sharper creases and neater models.

Bone folder

Various devices can be used to enhance folding. The so called 'bone folder' is a product used in the bookbinding industry. They can be used to enhance a crease by applying pressure along a fold. Although originally made from bone, they are now mainly plastic.

Chopsticks

A chopstick can be useful for manipulating the inside of a model, particularly to work on detail and create points.

Marker pen

Although the bone folder is designed specifically for folding, other everyday items such as marker pens can be used to press sharper creases.

Guillotine

Guillotines are good for cutting long straight lines. The design of the product enables cutting at right angles by aligning the paper's edge with the internal guide. The best cut can be achieved by pulling the cutting blade towards you and making a smooth single run.

Scissors

A good pair of scissors is invaluable for cutting paper. The best scissors for the task are those with long straight cutting blades.

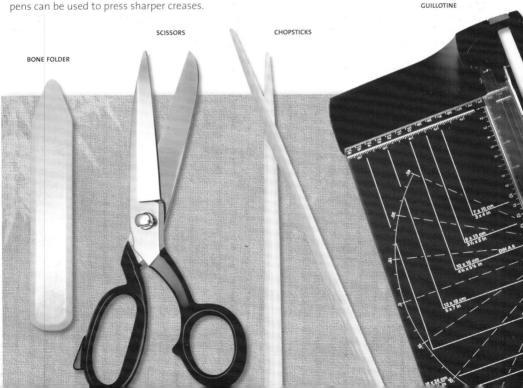

BONE FOLDER

SCISSORS

CHOPSTICKS

GUILLOTINE

Symbols

The diagrams in this book show a step by step construction process aided by the use of standard origami symbols listed below.

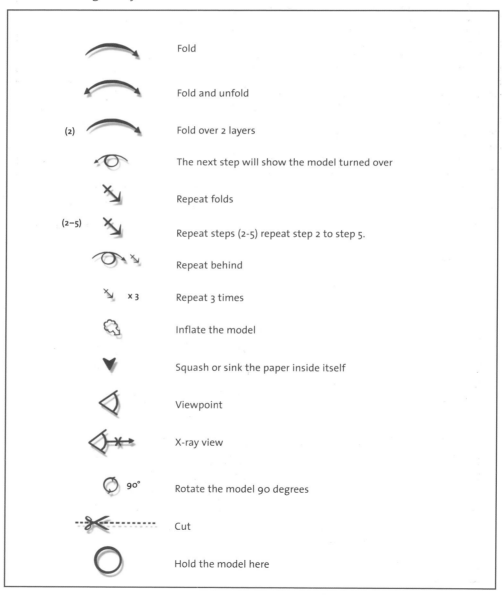

	Fold
	Fold and unfold
(2)	Fold over 2 layers
	The next step will show the model turned over
	Repeat folds
(2–5)	Repeat steps (2-5) repeat step 2 to step 5.
	Repeat behind
x 3	Repeat 3 times
	Inflate the model
	Squash or sink the paper inside itself
	Viewpoint
	X-ray view
90°	Rotate the model 90 degrees
	Cut
	Hold the model here

Folds

Origami instructions take you through a step by step process from start to finish. The process uses symbols to explain the transition from one step to the next. Each step shows how the folded project should look and it shows the folds that should be applied to move to the next step.

The challenge of origami diagrams is to explain the folding process. This is done by describing two possible folds. The valley fold creates a crease that folds away from the observer or makes a V shape. The mountain fold comes towards the observer and makes an opposite V shape. More advanced folds can be produced by combining these two folds.

The illustration below demonstrates mountain and valley folds. It also shows how arrows are used to describe the folding process.

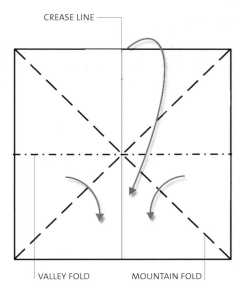

CREASE LINE

VALLEY FOLD   MOUNTAIN FOLD

arrows indicate the direction of the fold

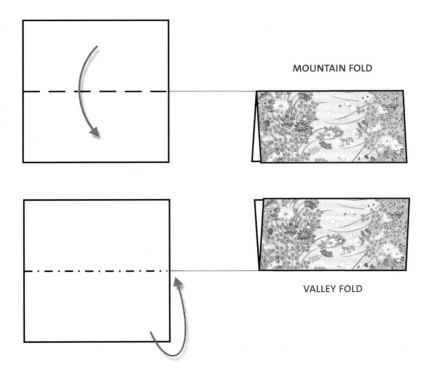

MOUNTAIN FOLD

VALLEY FOLD

Following instructions

Origami folding instructions can be tricky to follow, especially when there are several folds indicated by one diagram. The secret is to work methodically and carefully, paying attention not only to the step you are on but also looking ahead to the next.

The instructions are in two colours. The coloured side represents the front of the paper and the white side the underside. When using patterned paper, treat the coloured side as the patterned side. The diagrams for each design show the construction process broken down into steps that present one or two folds in the process. Each diagram shows a stage of the model and explains how to move to the next step. By following the numbered instructions you will be able to move through the steps and complete the project. Before attempting a step, make sure that the model

you are making looks like the step diagram. Look ahead to the next stage to see what the model will look like after the folds have been applied. Each step shows where to make each fold with either mountain or valley fold lines. Arrows indicate the direction of each fold. The caption below the diagram gives an extra commentary on the folds required for the step. When the step is completed the model should look like the image in the next step. If your model does not resemble the step stage you may have missed a fold, so try working back until you can match your model to a previous step.

example

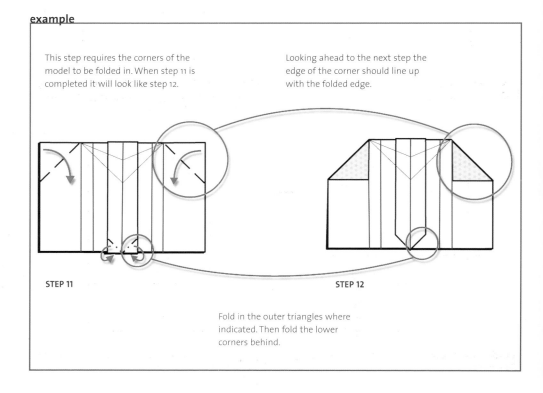

This step requires the corners of the model to be folded in. When step 11 is completed it will look like step 12.

Looking ahead to the next step the edge of the corner should line up with the folded edge.

STEP 11

STEP 12

Fold in the outer triangles where indicated. Then fold the lower corners behind.

Making a square

Folded models can be made from any shape of paper. However, origami is associated with folding paper squares and most of the projects in this book start from a square. You can buy pre-cut squares, or you can use the following technique to make a square from a rectangle.

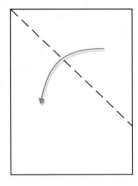

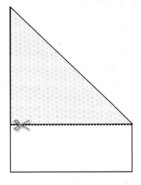

1 Fold over the top edge so that it aligns with the left edge of the paper.

2 Holding the folded edge to the paper, cut along the folded line using the folded edge as a ruler and separate the two parts.

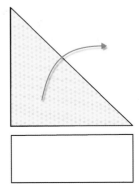

3 Unfold the folded edge and the square is ready for paper folding.

4 You now have a square and a residual rectangle which can also be used.

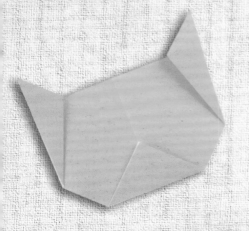

BASIC FOLDS

All the projects in this section are based on the mountain and valley folds. They are simple to create and are a good introduction to understanding the art of folding paper.

Basic folds

Paper folded models are typically explained using a series of step diagrams. These drawings explain how the paper should be folded using a set of standard symbols.

The two standard folds have been named mountain and valley folds. These folds manipulate the paper to cause the leading crease to come towards the observer or away, making a valley V shape, or a mountain, upside down V shape. If we look at the paper from the reverse side the shape of the folded form is reversed. If we were to perform a valley fold to a piece of paper the reverse side would show a mountain fold. More complex folds can be made by combining mountain and valley folds in one process and making the folds simultaneously. We will explore this later.

In this section we will introduce standard step folds that are used in origami notation and start to explore simple folds. All of the models in this section are made using either mountain or valley folds. We will also look at how diagrams help to explain the folding process and come to understand some of the basic symbols that are used in origami instructions.

folding tips

Follow the steps in numbered order, one at a time.

Look out for the reference points, both in the step you are trying to complete and also by looking ahead to see how the model should appear when the fold is completed.

Fold as accurately as possible. If the step requires you to fold the model in half, look around the fold and match the reference points indicated, align these points, then make the crease.

You should fold on a level surface. You can fold in the air but it is easier to make clean accurate folds when working on something stable and flat.

Make creases as sharply as possible. It may help to enhance creases by running a finger nail or other object along the folded edge.

folding paper in half

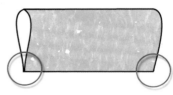

1 First of all line up the opposite sides and hold the edges together.

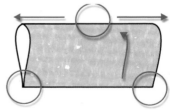

2 Hold the bottom two layers together. When the two layers are together pinch the middle and make the crease.

3 The paper is now accurately folded in half.

Cat's face

This is a simple model that demonstrates how, with just a few folds, a recognisable shape can be formed. The model is made from valley folds and introduces basic folds and instructions.

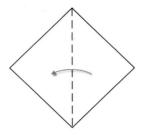

1 Fold the square in half diagonally.

2 Then fold the corner back to return to a flat square.

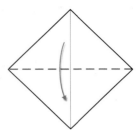

3 Fold the square in half diagonally again.

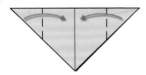

4 Fold the outer corners to the middle. This point can be found where the middle crease touches the top of the model.

5 Fold the top triangles to the edge and the lower corner up. The cat's face is complete.

CREASE LINE

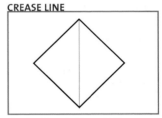

The hairline in the middle represents the crease made by the previous folds.

Cup

Moving on from the previous model we will introduce the mountain fold and show how it is used in diagrams. The mountain fold is the reverse of the valley fold.

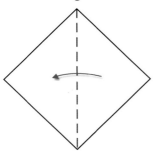

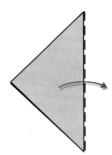

1 Start by folding the square in half diagonally.

2 Then fold the corner back to return to a flat square.

FOLD AND UNFOLD ARROW

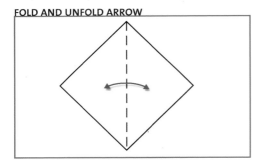

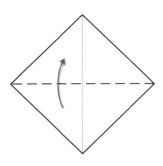

3 Steps 1 and 2 can be condensed into a single step fold and unfold.

4 Fold the square in half diagonally again and sharpen the crease.

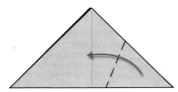

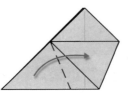

5 Fold the right corner to the left side. The corner should touch the edge and outer edge and is parallel to the base of the model.

6 Fold the left side corner over the folded point. Note the outer edge will align with the previously folded triangle.

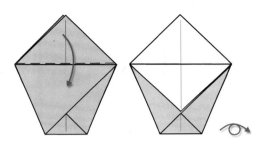

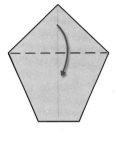

7 Fold the top triangle over the folded corners. Turn the model over.

8 Fold the top triangle over matching the fold you made behind. Open out the model slightly by gently squeezing either side. The cup is complete.

MOUNTAIN FOLD

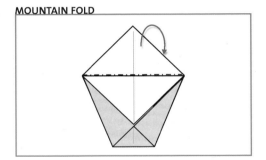

9 In steps 7 and 8 we turned the model over. This could have been explained by showing the corner being folded behind in step 7.

Mouse

The mouse shows how, with a few simple folds, an effective animal model can be produced. The model captures the basic features of a mouse. We will introduce rotating the model and repeating folds behind.

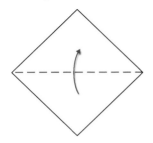

1 Fold the square in half diagonally.

2 Carefully fold the model in half as indicated.

3 Fold the lower corners to the middle.

4 Fold the lower edges to the middle.

5 Fold the top two corners of the model down.

6 Fold the top layer of the upper triangle down over the folded edges.

7 In the top section, fold the lower triangle up and fold over the tip of the lower layer.

8 Fold the model in half behind.

9 Rotate the model 90° clockwise.

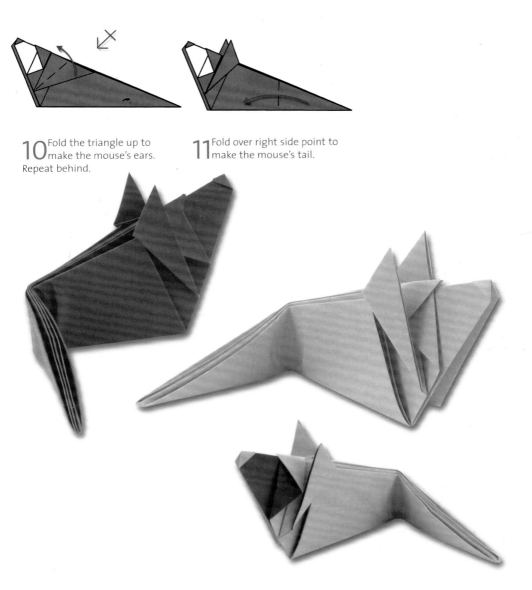

10 Fold the triangle up to make the mouse's ears. Repeat behind.

11 Fold over right side point to make the mouse's tail.

Shirt

This model shows how the features of an object can be captured in simple folds. For the shirt, these are the collar and sleeves. These instructions will introduce reference points which indicate how a fold should be made.

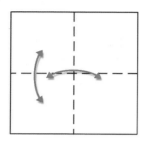

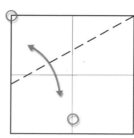

REFERENCE POINT

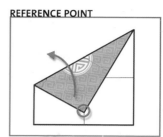

1 Start with a square. Fold in half horizontally and vertically.

2 Fold the top left corner down to touch the middle crease. The fold should start from the

top right corner. Then unfold. The point where the corner touches is called a reference point.

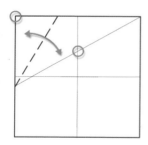

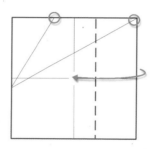

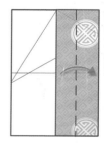

3 Fold the top left corner down to touch the crease made in the previous step. Then unfold.

4 Fold the left side over to touch the crease made in the previous step.

5 Fold the top edge back to the outer edge.

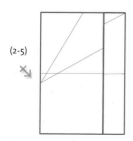

(2-5)

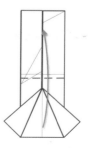

6 Repeat steps 2 to 5 on the other side.

7 Fold out the lower edges along the indicated lines.

8 Fold the lower section up. Leave a small gap at the top.

9 From the top section, fold down two triangles to start making the collar. Then turn over.

10 Fold the top corners into the model. This fold aligns with the previously folded triangles on the reverse. Turn over.

11 Fold over a small edge from the top to shape the collar. The shirt is complete.

Owl

This owl is slightly more complex. It is constructed using reference points and also some steps show more than one fold in a single process. We introduce the zigzag fold where the paper is folded up and down again.

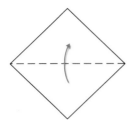

1 Start with a square. Fold in half vertically.

2 Fold the triangle in half again and unfold.

3 Fold the top triangle down to the middle of the lower edge. Then fold the triangle back.

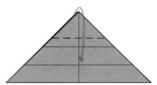

4 Fold the lower edge up to the crease made in the previous step. Then fold it back again.

5 Fold the top two layers down to the intersection of the crease made in the previous step and the middle crease.

6 Fold the top layer back up. The tip of the triangle should extend beyond the upper edge beneath.

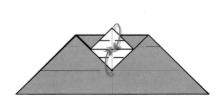

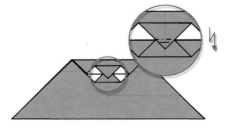

7 Fold both the corners in. The lower corner should be beneath the top corner.

8 Fold the top corner underneath and then out again. See the pull out detail above.

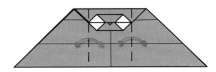

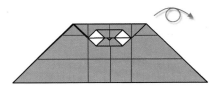

9 Fold the outside corners in and out again. These folds should touch the folded section above.

10 Now turn the model over to work on the reverse side.

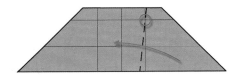

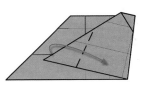

11 Fold the right corner in along a slight diagonal. This fold should pass through the point where the upper creases cross.

12 Now fold the corner back to the right, again along a slight diagonal.

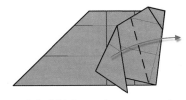

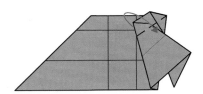

13 Carefully fold the top layer over as shown by the arrow above.

14 As neatly as possible fold over the top corner of the model.

Owl continued

(11-14)

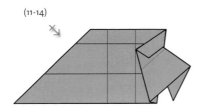 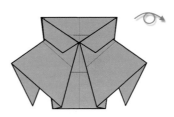

15 Repeat steps 11 to 14 on the other side. This should mirror the folds already completed.

16 Then turn the model over to add the final folds for the detail.

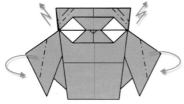

17 Fold the edges of the wings behind. Then shape the ears by folding the top triangles behind and back again.

Face

The face uses the basic mountain and valley folds. It introduces more flexible folding where reference points are used as a guide to where a fold should be made, rather than a rule. This enables the folder to interpret the design to their own taste.

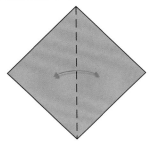

1 Start with a square piece of paper. Neatly fold in half vertically, then unfold.

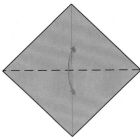

2 Now fold the square in half horizontally and unfold.

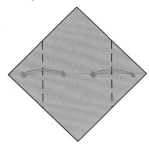

3 Fold the outer corners to the middle. Then unfold them both.

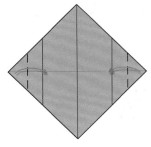

4 Fold the outer corners in. The tips of these folds should extend slightly beyond the crease made in the previous step.

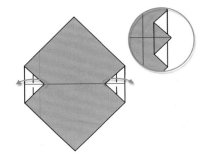

5 Fold out the triangles again. The tips of the folded triangles should extend beyond the edge of the triangle beneath.

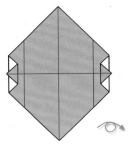

6 Then turn the model over left to right as indicated.

Face continued

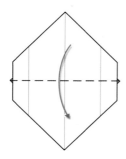

7 Now, as accurately as you can, fold the model in half vertically.

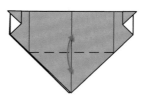

8 Fold and unfold the lower triangle to make a crease, indicated by the dotted line.

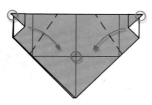

9 Fold the outer corners in. The tips should touch the crease shown by the reference point.

10 Fold the top layer of the lower point up to the centre of the model.

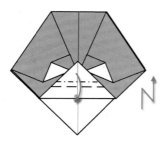

11 Fold the layer down and back up again. This zigzag fold is shown by the symbol to the right of the model.

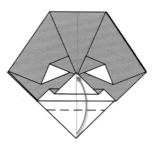

12 Fold the lower triangle up to touch the centre of the model.

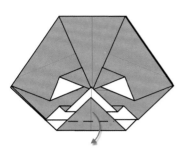

13 Fold the triangle down again. The fold should align with the edge beneath.

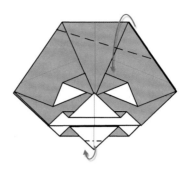

14 Fold the top corners over to start to form hair. Fold the lower tip behind.

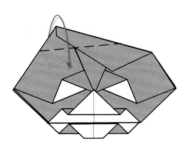

15 Fold the left top corner over to form an indication of hair.

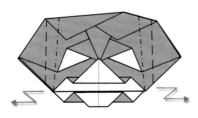

16 Fold the outer corners behind and out again to form the ears.

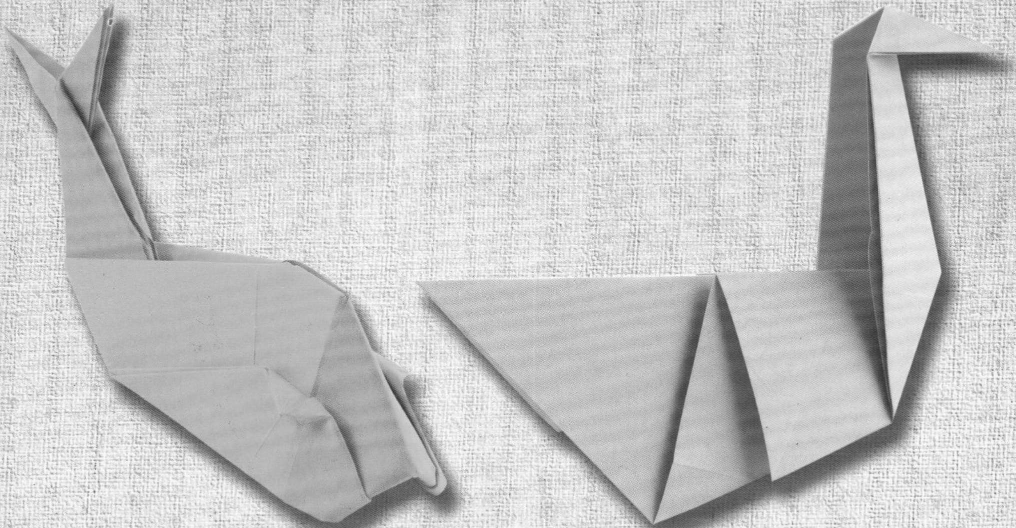

BASIC TECHNIQUES

In this section we will introduce more advanced folds and also bases. The sequence of folds has been structured to gradually introduce more to our folding toolkit such as the reverse fold, the squash fold, the bird's foot fold and the crimp. We will also introduce bases. These form a good foundation to understanding origami design. We then demonstrate how the folds or bases can be used in a completed model.

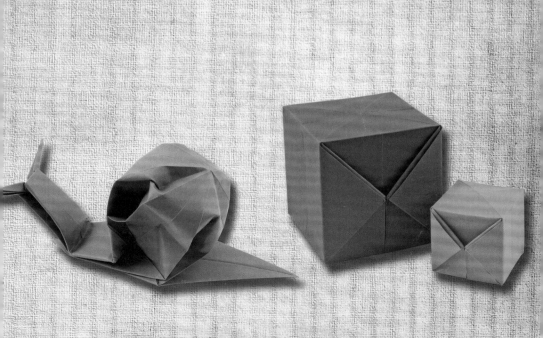

Swan

This is a simple traditional model. The diagrams show two ways to make the model and will explain the reverse fold. Start with a square, coloured side up.

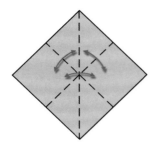

1 Fold and unfold the square in half lengthwise and again diagonally.

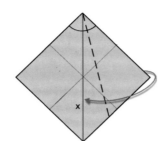

2 Fold the right hand corner to the middle line crease marked with X. This is a reference point.

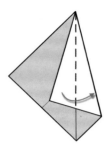

3 Fold the corner back again along the indicated line.

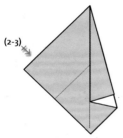

4 Repeat steps 2 to 3 on the left side.

5 Fold the top point down as neatly as possible.

6 Fold the point back up again along the line indicated.

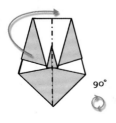

7 Fold the model in half behind and rotate.

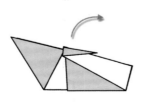

8 Hold the model where indicated and fold up the head and neck.

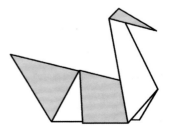

9 The swan is complete. This method employs the easy way to make a reverse fold.

Reverse folds

inside reverse fold

1 Start from swan step 4. Fold the model in half behind.

2 Inside reverse folds are made by using a mountain fold to the front and rear of a point.

3 This will reverse the top of the point inside the model.

outside reverse fold

1 Applying a valley fold to the front and rear will cause the point to reverse outside.

2 Turn the top of the point inside out.

Preliminary base

This base is the first fold in many origami designs. It is made by combining mountain and valley folds into one process. Start with a square coloured side up.

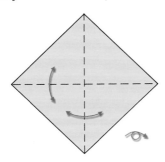

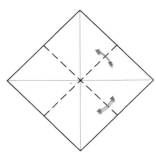

1 Fold and unfold the square in half vertically and horizontally. Then turn over.

2 Fold and unfold the square in half along both diagonal lines indicated.

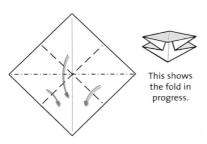

This shows the fold in progress.

3 Re-fold the folds made in steps 1 and 2. This will bring all of the corners together.

4 This is how the finished preliminary base should look.

Star box

The star box is a simple design that starts with a preliminary base. With this project we will introduce a new procedure, the squash fold.

1 Start with a preliminary base. Rotate 180°. Fold the outside edges in to the middle crease.

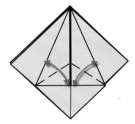 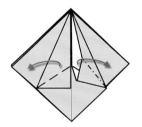 

2 Fold and unfold the corners to the folded edge.

3 Fold over one edge of the folded corner and flatten. This will cause a squash fold.

4 Fold the edges on both sides behind as shown.

(2-5)

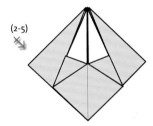

5 Repeat steps 2 to 5 on the other side (behind).

6 Crease the base. Then fold over the front and back points. Pull the folded corners apart and shape the base.

Waterbomb base

This waterbomb base applies a similar technique to the preliminary base. However, the process is applied to the model squarely rather than diagonally. Start with a square coloured side up.

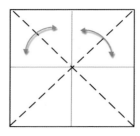

1 Fold and unfold the square in half lengthwise. Now turn over.

2 Fold and unfold the square in half and diagonally.

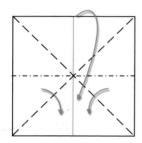

This shows the fold in progress.

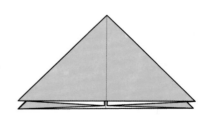

3 Re-fold the folds made in steps 1 and 2. This will bring all of the corners together.

4 This is how the finished waterbomb base should look.

Waterbomb

The waterbomb is another simple design and with this project we will introduce a new procedure, inflating the model.

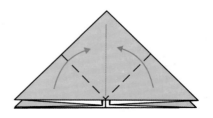

1 Fold the corners to the centre line as neatly as possible, keep the folds sharp.

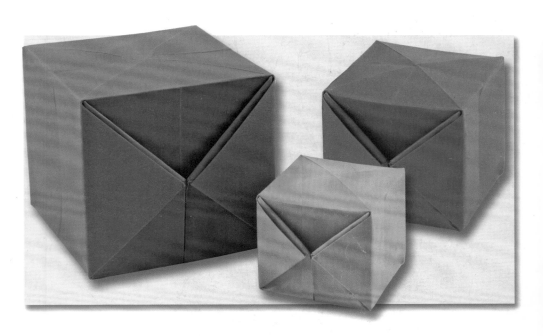

2 Crease the centre line as accurately as you can.

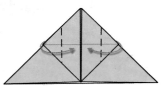

3 Fold the corners in to the middle crease line.

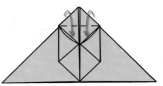

4 Fold the top corners into the model.

(5-9)

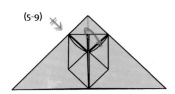

5 Tuck the folded corner into the pocket. Do this on both sides. Repeat steps 5 to 9 behind.

6 Crease the top and bottom corners.

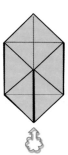

7 To complete, inflate the model by blowing gently into the hole at the bottom.

Bird base

The bird base is so called as it is the foundation for the traditional Japanese models, the flapping bird and the crane. Start with a preliminary base (see page 36).

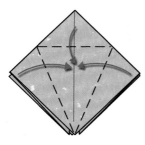

1 Fold in the outside edges to the middle. Then fold over the top triangle.

2 Sharpen the edges of the folds then unfold all the folds made in the previous step.

3 Fold the front layer up along the crease made in the previous step.

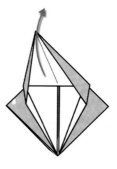

4 Fold the front layer up and then flatten. This will close the flaps either side to the middle crease.

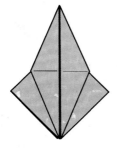

5 Repeat steps 1 to 4 behind. Try to be as accurate as possible making this mirror the other side.

6 The bird base is now complete and should look like this.

Flapping bird

The flapping bird is a traditional action model and when complete you can pull its tail to make the wings flap.

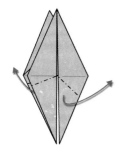 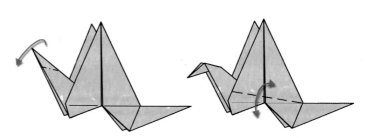

1 Start with a bird base. Reverse fold the left and right sides.

2 Reverse fold the left hand point to form the head.

3 Crease the wing where indicated. Repeat behind. The bird is complete.

Flapping the wings

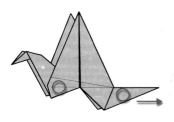

1 Hold the model as indicated by the 'O's. Pull the tail gently.

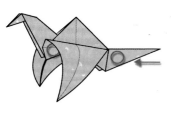

2 The wings should flap. Reversing the previous movement will return the wings to their upright position.

Crane

This is the most traditional Japanese origami model created using the bird base.
Legend has it that if you make a thousand cranes your wishes will come true.

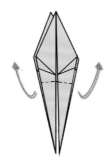

1 Start with a bird base. On one side fold the edges to the middle. Repeat behind.

2 Reverse fold the points into the model.

3 Reverse fold the left hand point to form the head.

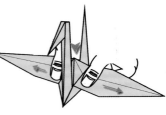

4 Fold both the wings down, make sure that they are of equal length.

5 Hold the wings and gently open the body, by pulling each wing outwards.

Frog base

The frog base is another way of folding a preliminary base. The distribution of paper is different to the bird base as a result of the application of squash folds to the edges of the preliminary base.

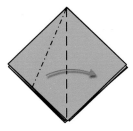

1 Start with a preliminary base. Raise one corner and squash.

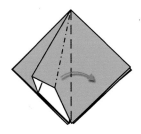

2 This shows the squash fold in progress.

3 Fold both the edges to the middle crease line.

4 Unfold the folds made in step 3.

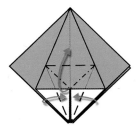

5 Fold up the edge along the middle. This will reverse the folds made in step 3.

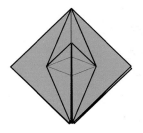

6 Repeat steps 1 to 5 on the other three corners.

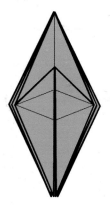

7 The frog base is complete and should look like this.

Snail

The snail is a traditional design using the frog base. It demonstrates the paper distribution as the shell is formed from the middle of the square.

1 Start with a frog base. Fold down the flaps on all sides of the model.

2 Fold over the front and back layers. Keep the creases accurate and sharp.

3 Carefully fold the lower front point up to meet the top point.

4 Fold the edges of the front layer behind and then turn the model over.

5 Fold the tip of the front lower point of the snail behind.

6 Now neatly fold over two layers along the line of the centre crease as indicated.

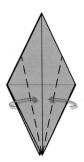

7 Fold the two outer edges in to the middle. The next stages need to be folded neatly.

8 Fold the left side top layer over to the right side of the model.

9 Carefully fold over two layers of the snail to the right.

10 Now repeat steps 7 to 10 on the left side, making sure not to miss any layers.

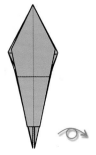

11 Now turn the model over to add the finishing touches to the snail.

12 Fold up the two lower points in order to form the snail's antenna.

Snail continued

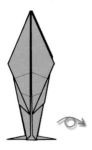

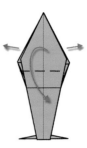

13 Check that you have finished folding all the layers properly and then turn the model over.

14 Fold the point up and open out the layers. This will round the shell.

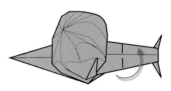

15 Continue to open out the shell. Don't pull it as the act of opening the layers will form the shell. Now rotate the model.

16 Now you are looking at a side view of the snail. Fold up the neck slightly, to an angle of about 45°. The snail is complete.

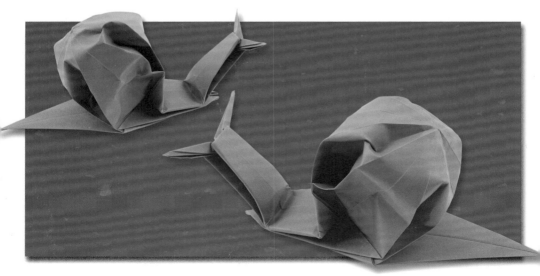

Fish base

The fish base is formed in a process where a mountain and valley fold are made at the same time.

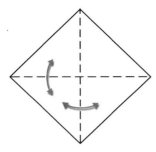

1 Start with a square sheet of paper. Fold and unfold the square in half diagonally.

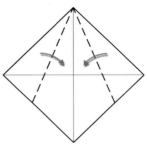

2 Fold both the edges in to align with the crease in the centre of the paper.

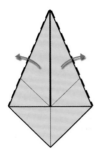

3 Sharpen the crease and then fold both the triangles back out again.

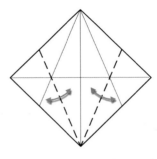

4 Fold and unfold the lower edges to the middle. This is the mirror of steps 2 and 3.

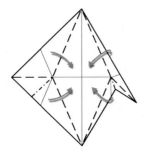

5 Fold in the lower and upper edges to the middle together. The right side shows this process in action. This is sometimes called a rabbit ear.

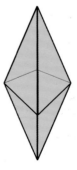

6 Now neatly fold over two layers along the line of the centre crease as indicated.

Fish

The fish base is named as it converts a square into a shape that resembles a fish and is the foundation for many other origami fish patterns.

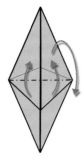

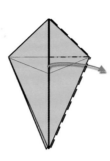

1 Fold the top point behind and the front triangles up.

2 Open up the paper on the right hand side.

3 Fold the left side over and tuck the top triangle into the right, fold the layers together.

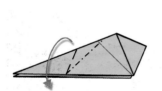

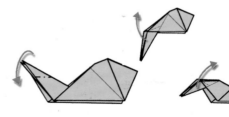

4 Reverse fold the triangle down and then fold it up again. This is called a bird's foot.

5 Reverse fold the two layers of the tail.

6 Fold the inner layer back out again.

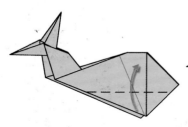

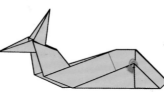

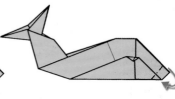

7 Fold the front corner up. Repeat behind.

8 Fold the tip of the triangle down to make an eye.

9 Reverse fold the front of the fish along the lines shown to form the mouth.

bird's foot

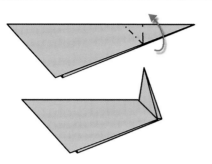

The bird's foot combines a mountain and valley fold by folding the point down and up again.

crimp fold

The crimp fold combines a mountain and valley fold. The final result is that the point is rotated slightly.

Sink fold

The sink fold reverses paper inside. This exercise will demonstrate the fold using a preliminary base.

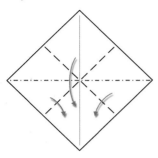

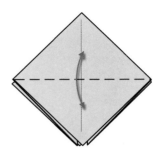

1 Fold the corners into the middle to make a preliminary base (see page 36).

2 Fold and unfold vertically along the crease in the centre of the model.

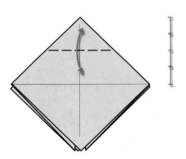

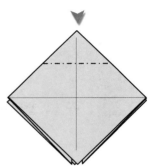

3 Fold and unfold the top tip to the fold made in the previous step.

4 The sink fold reverses the tip of the paper back into the model.

the sink fold

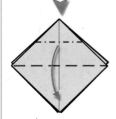

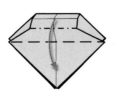

Fold over the middle and reverse the fold above. Continue the fold and open the paper above. Flatten the top section. Fold the edge back up and refold the sides up again. The sink fold is complete.

Coaster

The coaster is a model made around a sink fold. Start with a preliminary base with a sink procedure applied to the top section.

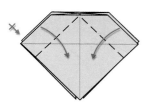

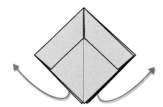

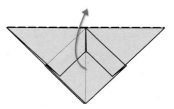

1 Fold the top edges into the middle. Repeat behind.

2 Reverse fold out the middle layers on both sides.

3 Fold up the front layer. This will cause the sink fold to open out. Flatten the model.

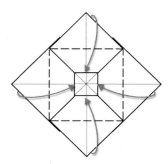

4 Fold the edges into the middle. Tuck these under the flattened sink fold.

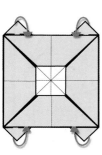

5 Fold the corners over and under the front layer.

Blinz bases

Blinzing is a technique where the corners of the square are folded into the middle at the start of the folding process. This technique can be applied to other bases to form more complex shapes.

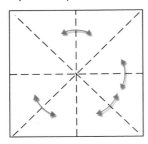

1 Fold and unfold the square in half vertically, horizontally and diagonally.

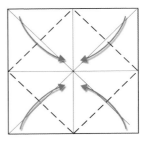

2 Fold the corners as accurately as you can into the middle of the paper.

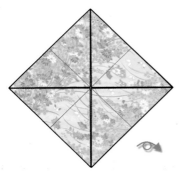

3 The model will look like this, with all four corners neatly folded into the centre now turn over.

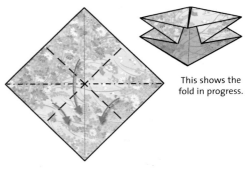

This shows the fold in progress.

5 Re-fold the folds made in step 1 to form a preliminary base.

6 Sharpen all the creases and the blinz preliminary base is complete.

Box

This project is a traditional Japanese box created using a blinzed preliminary base.

1 Start with a blinzed preliminary base. Rotate 180°.

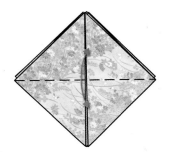

2 Fold and unfold the top corner.

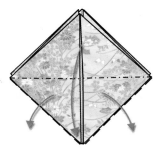

3 Re-fold the fold made in step 2 and open out the two sides.

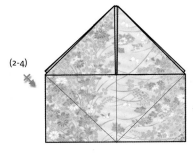

(2-4)

4 Open out the flaps and flatten the opened paper, smooth the creases.

5 Repeat steps 2 to 4 behind. Making sure that this exactly matches the other side.

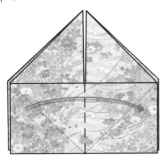

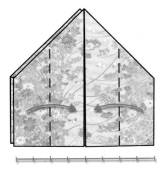

6 Fold the front layer over, from left to right. Keep the fold parallel to the centre line.

7 Carefully fold the two outer edges in to meet at the centre creaseline.

Box continued

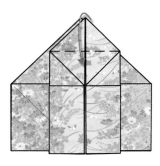

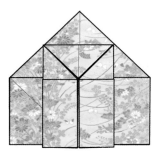

8 Fold the top corner over to meet the line as indicated.

9 Repeat steps 7 to 8 behind, making sure that the folds are accurate.

10 Fold over the top flaps perpendicular to the model.

11 Hold the flaps and gently pull apart. Then shape the box.

Crease patterns

If we fold and unfold an origami model we can see a pattern caused by the folds. This is called a crease pattern. It is possible to construct an origami model using a crease pattern. There are also more advanced design techniques that evolve origami models directly from crease patterns.

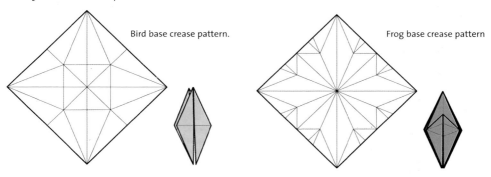

Bird base crease pattern.

Frog base crease pattern

More blinz folds

The blinz technique can also be applied to other bases. This process duplicates the structure of the original bases and leads to the creation of more complex structures. The conventional bases develop points from the corners of a square. The blinz process enables additional points to be developed from the edges of the square. The blinz bird and frog bases create an eight pointed base.

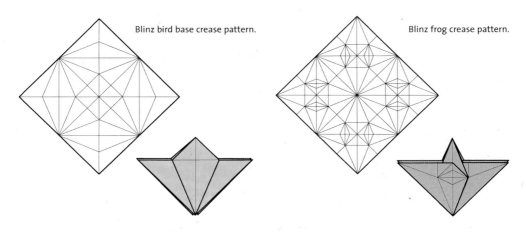

Blinz bird base crease pattern.

Blinz frog crease pattern.

ALL SHAPES AND SIZES

Classic origami is associated with folding a square. However, folding principles can be applied to any shaped piece of paper. In this section we explore models made from rectangles, hexagons and strips of paper. It is possible to fold any shaped piece of paper.

Hat

The hat is a simple traditional model. You can make it from a large rectangle such as a sheet of newspaper or you can use wrapping paper for a more colourful model.

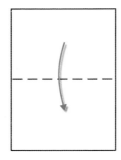

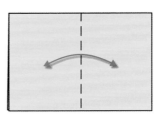

1 Start with rectangle. Fold it in half along the longest side

2 Now fold and unfold along to form a crease down the middle.

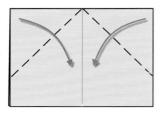

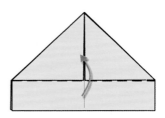

3 Fold the top left and right corners neatly in to meet the middle crease.

4 Fold the lower edge up over the folded triangles.

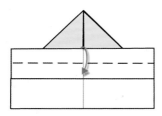

5 Fold the edge down again. Turn the hat over and repeat on the other side.

Printer's hat

The printer's hat is slightly more complex. It is so called as its origin has been traced to the printing industry where workers would make them from newspaper when working in dusty conditions.

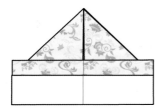

1 Start with step 5 of the traditional hat (page 58). Turn the model over.

2 Fold the left and right edges in to the middle crease line.

3 Fold the top corner in and tuck it beneath the folded layers below.

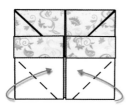

4 Fold the lower corners to align with the folded edge.

5 Now fold the lower corner up to the folded edge.

6 Fold the lower corner up. Tuck in under the folded edge above.

7 Fold the front layer of the pocket up. This causes the edges to fold in. Flatten the model.

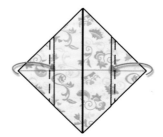

8 Fold the edges in and tuck them under the folded edge in the middle.

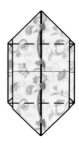

9 Fold and unfold the top and bottom corners to the middle crease.

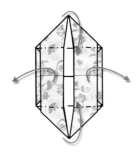 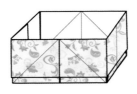 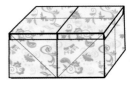

10 Fold the edges out to form a box shape.

11 Smooth out the box until it is a neat square shape.

12 Turn the box over and the hat is complete.

Stunt plane

The stunt plane is a traditional flying model. It can be adjusted to perform loops and turns by adding flaps on the rear of each wing.

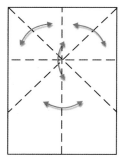

1 Start with an A4 rectangle. Fold in half lengthwise. Fold the top section as shown.

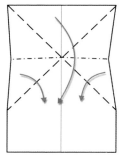

2 Fold the top section into a waterbomb base.

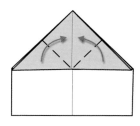

3 Fold the lower corners of the waterbomb shape to the middle crease line.

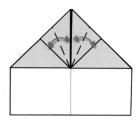

4 In the top section, fold and unfold each of the edges to the middle.

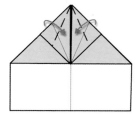

5 In the top section, Fold the outer edges to the middle.

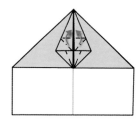

6 In the top section, fold the corners up. This will cause the lower edges to fold in. This process is similar to a fish base.

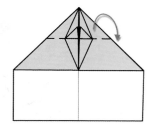

7 Fold the top corner down behind as indicated.

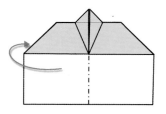

8 Fold the model in half by folding the edge behind. Then rotate the model 90°.

9 Fold the wing down along the dotted line.

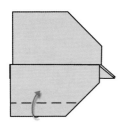

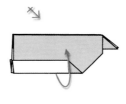
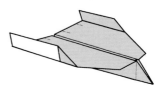

10 Fold the edge of the wing up. Repeat steps 9 to 10 behind.

11 Fold the wings at the front and behind up perpendicular to the model.

12 The stunt plane is complete. You can add flaps along the dotted lines on both wings.

Star

The star is made from a strip of paper. It shows an interesting folding technique that creates a pentagon and an enclosed space. The final step demonstrates an interesting technique to make the model three dimensional.

1 Start with a strip of paper at least 4 x 1 in proportion. Take one end behind the other, but take care not to fold or crease it.

2 Move the lower end over the top part.

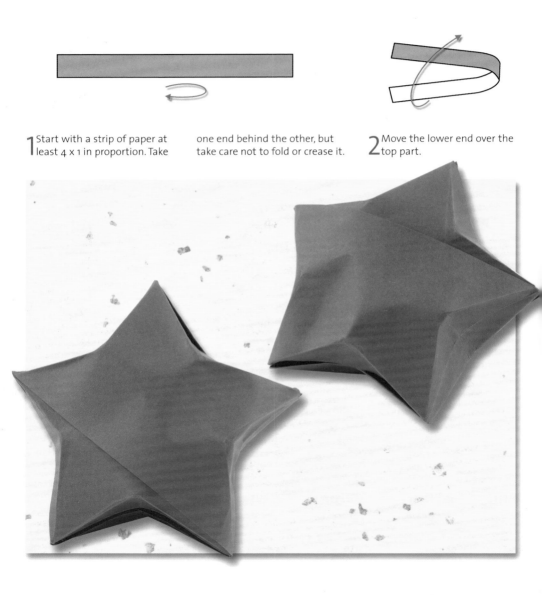

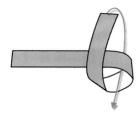

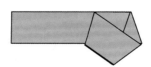

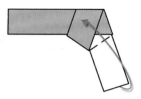

3 Pass the end in underneath the lower part of the strip.

4 Pull the lower edge resulting in a paper knot.

5 Fold the end of the strip up. Do not crease it.

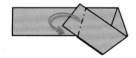

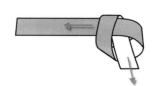

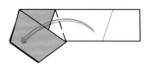

6 Tuck the end of the strip into the layer beneath.

7 It should look like this now. Turn the model over.

8 Fold the strip of paper over, along the edge of the folded paper beneath.

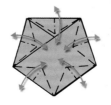

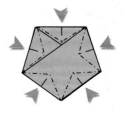

9 Fold the strip of paper over, along the edge of the folded paper beneath.

10 The folded strip now forms a pentagon. Fold and unfold the edges in to make a star shape.

11 Reverse fold the creases from step 10 to make a 3D star.

Hexagon

Although classic origami models start from a square, other shapes can be folded. In this exercise we will use a square to make a hexagon that can be used to make the next project, a six-petalled flower.

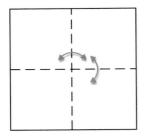

1 Start with a square, coloured side down. Fold and unfold in half vertically and horizontally.

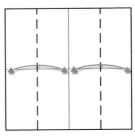

2 Fold and unfold the left and right edges to the middle crease line.

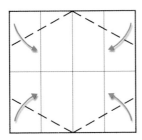

3 Fold the outer corners in to the quarter creases. The fold starts from the middle crease.

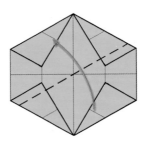

4 Fold up the lower right edge to align with the upper left edge.

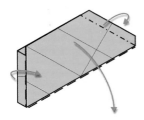

5 Fold the left edge over the folded edge. Fold the right edge over the folded edge behind. Then unfold to a square.

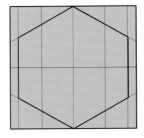

6 The inner creases within the square form a regular hexagon.

Flower

The flower can be made from any regular polygon, including a square. This version is made from a hexagon. A hexagon can be made by cutting around the inner creases from the previous exercise.

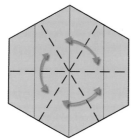

1 Start with a hexagon. Fold and unfold opposite edges together. Rotate the model slightly.

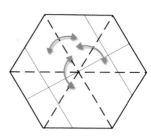

2 Fold the model in half three times between the corners of the hexagon.

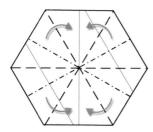

3 Fold along the creases made in the previous steps. This process is similar to the waterbomb and preliminary bases but applied to a hexagon.

4 Fold up and squash the point as indicated in the diagram.

5 Fold and unfold the edges of the squashed point to the middle crease.

6 Fold the paper down between the creases made previously. This will cause the edges to fold in.

Flower continued

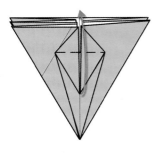

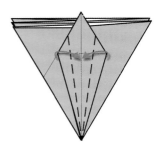

7 Now take the point you have just created in the previous step and fold it back up.

8 Fold the edges of the centre shape in to the middle crease line.

9 Now repeat steps 4 to 8 carefully on all of the other corners.

10 Fold the six corners out and start to shape the flower.

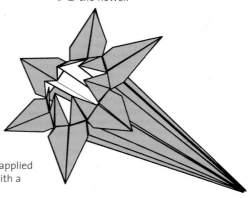

11 The six-petalled flower is made from a hexagon. This folding procedure can be applied to any regular polygon. Try experimenting with a triangle, square or pentagon.

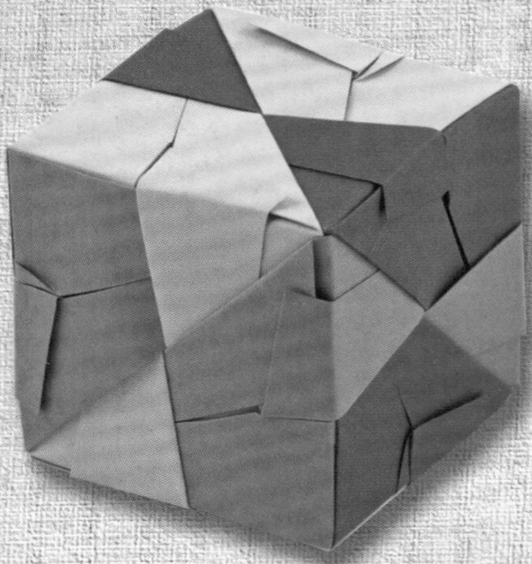

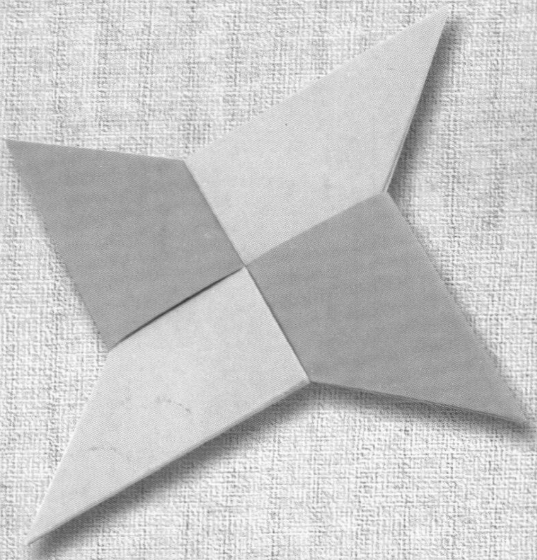

MODULAR ORIGAMI

Modular origami involves using multiple units to create more complex constructions. In this section we will explore three different projects. The Ninja star is a traditional design and involves making two units that weave together. The pagoda involves making modular sections for each layer of the building. The final project is to create geometric shapes from simple units. The shape of the unit enables them to be assembled at different angles to create three-dimensional shapes.

Ninja star

The Ninja star is made from two units that are mirrors of each other woven together. The model uses two 2 x 1 rectangles which can be made by cutting a square in half.

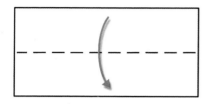

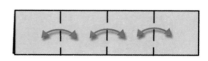

1 Start with a 2 x 1 rectangle. Fold in half lengthwise.

2 Fold in half and then in half again to make creases that divide the rectangle into quarters.

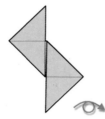

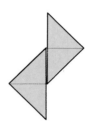

3 For one of the segments fold the left side up and the right side down.

4 Sharpen all the creases and then turn the segment over.

5 Segment one is complete and looks like this.

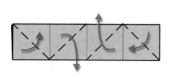

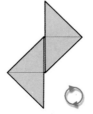

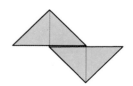

6 For the other segment fold the left side down and the right side up. This reverses the folds in the other segment.

7 Smooth all the creases and then rotate the segment 90°.

8 Segment two is now complete and should look like this.

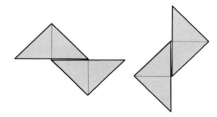

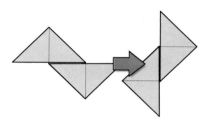

9 Take the two segments and line them up as shown above.

10 Place segment two on top of segment one where indicated.

11 Fold over the points on the lower segment. Tuck the ends of the points into the upper segment.

12 Turn over the linked segments.

13 Fold over the points on the lower segment. Tuck the ends of the points into the upper segment.

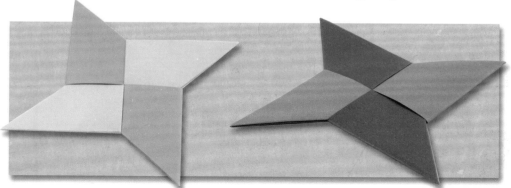

Pagoda

The pagoda is a traditional model that explores modular origami techniques by making a series of units. The units are different layers of the pagoda structure. Make several and build the pagoda as high as you like.

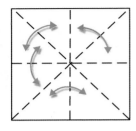

1 Fold and unfold the square in half and diagonally.

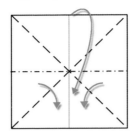

2 Re-fold the creases to make a waterbomb base.

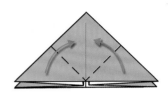

3 Now neatly fold the outer corners up.

4 Fold down the folded corners, open them out and flatten.

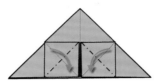

5 Fold the corners behind and into the model.

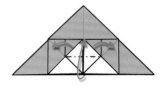

6 Fold the edges of the top layer out. This will cause the lower layer to fold up. Then flatten.

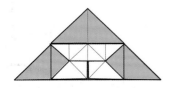

7 Turn the model over and repeat steps 3 to 6 behind.

8 Fold over one layer. Repeat behind.

9 Fold the edges in to the middle. Repeat behind.

10 Fold over one layer.
Repeat behind.

11 The pagoda segment is
now complete.

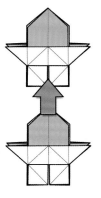

12 Two segments will fit
together by inserting
the top of one into the base
of another.

13 Adding several units will
make a taller pagoda. The
layers can be made of variable
sizes so that it tapers towards
the top. This can be achieved by
using several different size
squares of paper to start with.

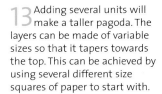

Geometric unit

This project develops a unit that can be combined to create three-dimensional shapes. The unit is based on two isosceles triangles, and it has points and pockets that can be woven together to create more complex shapes.

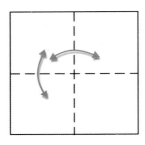

1 Fold and unfold a square across the middle both horizontally and vertically.

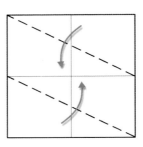

2 Make two diagonal folds between the corner and the middle crease.

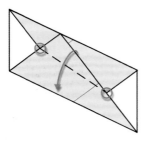

3 Fold over the corner where the top layers meet. Repeat this on the other folded corner.

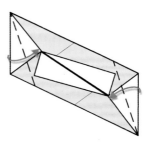

4 Fold the edges in to the section folded made in the previous step.

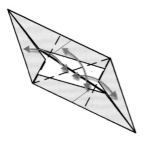

5 Fold and unfold the outer triangles diagonally along the middle.

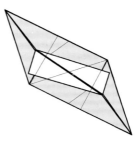

6 The unit is now complete and should look like this.

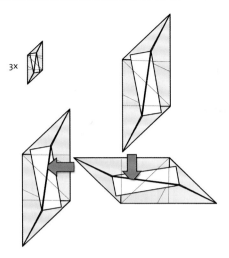

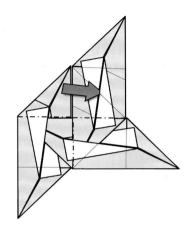

7 Make three units of the same size and orientation. The units can be assembled by inserting corners of one unit into the central pocket of another.

8 Three units are now linked. Now insert the remaining corner into the associated pocket. This will transform the flat surface into a 3D pyramid.

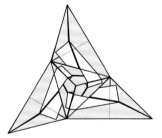

9 Turn the assembled units over and repeat the process of inserting points into pockets.

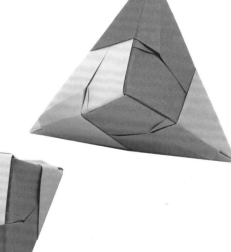

10 Three units assembled. This is called a hexahedron.

Geometric unit continued

3X

HEXAHEDRON
Three units assembled. This is called a hexahedron.

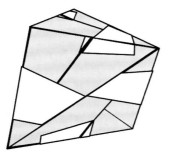

6X

CUBE
Six units assembled. This is a cube.

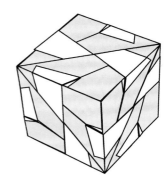

12X

STELLATED OCTAHEDRON
Twelve units assembled. This is a stellated octahedron.

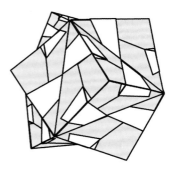

30X

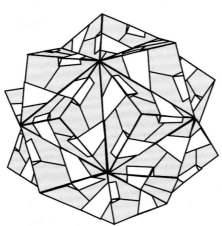

STELLATED ICOSAHEDRON
Thirty units assembled. This is a stellated icosahedron.

ADVANCED PROJECTS

The advanced projects feature some more complex designs that incorporate many of the folding techniques we have previously explored. The most complex model in this section is the elephant. It starts with half a blinzed frog base, for the front of the animal. The back of the elephant will show you how to fold in a more freeform style that moves away from the rigid design of the classic origami bases.

Heart

Hearts are a popular subject in origami. This model uses some of the techniques from the pentagonal star. The model is based around a flat heart shape that can be popped out to make it three dimensional.

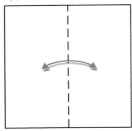

1 Fold and unfold the square coloured side down. Fold in half lengthwise.

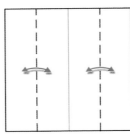

2 Fold and unfold the edges to the middle.

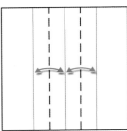

3 Fold and unfold between the folds made in the previous two steps.

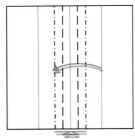

4 Mountain fold the folds in step 2 and fold them to the middle of the piece.

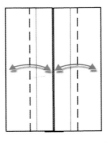

5 Fold and unfold the edges of the model to the middle.

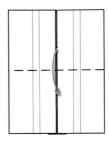

6 Fold the model in half along the indicated line.

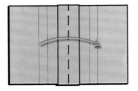

7 Fold the model in half along the dotted line.

8 Fold over the top left corner to the middle crease.

9 Fold and unfold the corner to align with the crease made in the previous step.

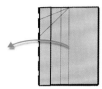

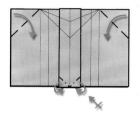

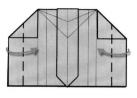

10 Now unfold the top layer to the left.

11 Fold in the outer triangles where indicated. Then fold the lower corners behind. Repeat behind.

12 Fold both the edges in along the indicated line.

13 Fold the lower corners in and tuck them under the pleated middle layer.

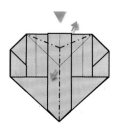

14 Push the top triangle in and 3D the model.

Angel

The angel uses simple folding techniques to make the model but there is one complex move when making the head.

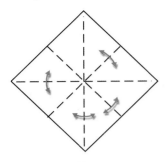

1 Fold and unfold the square in half lengthwise and diagonally.

2 Fold the square in half diagonally. Fold the outer edges in and out again.

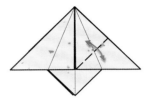

3 Fold the right corner up and back again.

4 Fold the triangle up. This will make the crease made in step 3 touch the middle.

5 Fold the top right edge down. This will cause the layer beneath to fold.

6 Fold the top layer back up again.

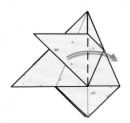

7 Fold the triangle back over left to right.

(4-8)

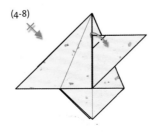

8 Fold over a small corner to lock the folds. Repeat steps 4 to 8 on the other side.

9 Fold the lower triangle into the model. Repeat behind.

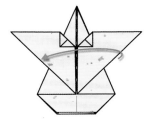

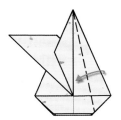

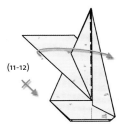

(11-12)

10 Fold the right side over to the left.

11 Fold the right side edge into the middle.

12 Fold the edge over. Repeat steps 11 to 12 behind.

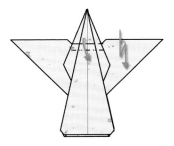

13 Turn over, then fold the top triangle down and up again. Pull the layers in the triangle out to shape the face.

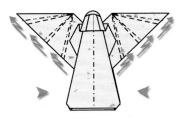

14 Crimp fold the wings to create a texture. Round the body slightly.

Dragon

This project uses the bird base to make a mythical creature. It uses an interesting technique to model the legs and wings.

1 Start with a bird base (see page 40). Fold the top points down on the front layer and then behind.

2 Sink fold the top corner. Fold up the two inner points.

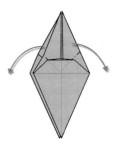

3 Reverse fold the two points. Note the different levels of the folds.

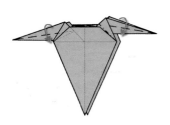

4 Narrow the left and right reversed points along the lines indicated.

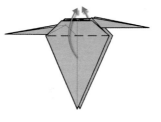

5 Fold up the lower points at the front and behind.

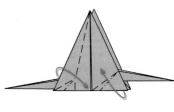

6 Fold the front side of the triangle over making a rabbit ear fold and then fold the back corner up.

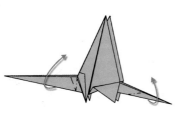

7 Crimp the left point up and then reverse fold the right point up.

8 Fold the left point back and back again. This is sometimes called a bird's foot fold.

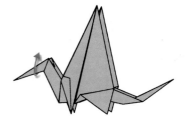

9 Fold out the trapped paper at the front and behind.

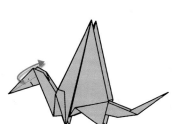

10 Reverse fold the point, to start forming the head.

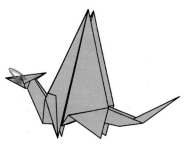

11 Fold the edges over at the front and behind.

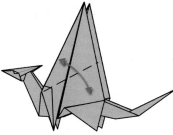

12 Slide the folded section of the head up a little.

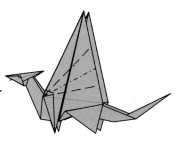

13 Fold the corners of the head up on both sides.

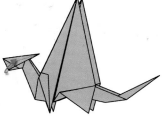

14 Fold the edge of the triangle over to make eyes. Repeat behind to complete the head.

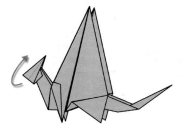

15 Fold and unfold the middle of the wing.

16 Fold the wing in and out again to make a fan shape.

Elephant

This is a much more complex project. Starting off with half a blinzed frog base, it also requires the use of sink and crimp folds.

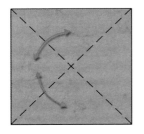

1 Fold and unfold the square diagonally.

2 Fold the corners to the middle. Then turn the model over.

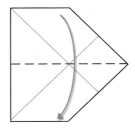

3 Now accurately fold the model in half.

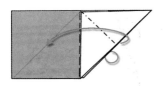

4 Fold over the right corner. Raise and squash the point.

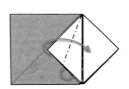

5 Raise and squash the point you have just made.

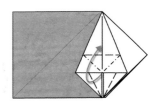

6 Fold the edge up and reverse the edges together. This method is used when creating the frog base.

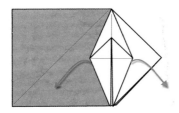

7 Unfold the model. Leave the folded corner folded.

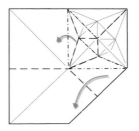

8 Refold the folds where indicated. This will create a blinzed frog base.

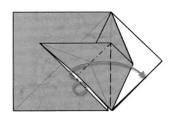

9 Raise as indicated and squash the point.

(6-11)

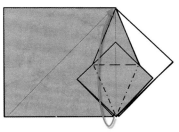

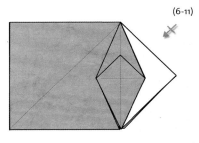

10 Fold the squashed point up to make a bird base shape.

11 Fold the corner down. Then repeat steps 6 to 11 behind.

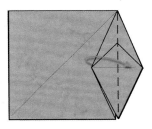

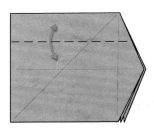

12 Fold the edge over. Now turn over and repeat the fold behind.

13 Fold and unfold the edge over to the middle as indicated by the dotted line.

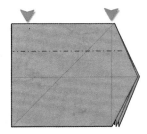

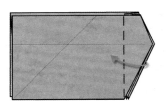

14 Make a sink fold along the crease made in step 13.

15 Fold the edge back over. Turn over and repeat behind.

Elephant continued

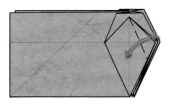

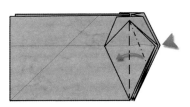

16 Fold and unfold the edge to the middle. Repeat behind.

17 Fold up the front corner and squash along the folds made in step 16. Repeat behind.

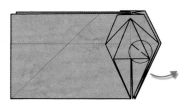

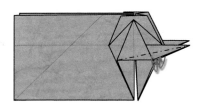

18 Reverse fold up the point. Turn the model over and repeat behind.

19 Fold the edges of the folded point behind on the front and behind.

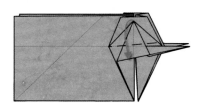

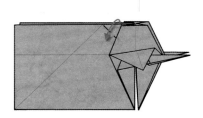

20 Fold the triangle down along the line indicated and then repeat behind.

21 Fold the corner just behind the head. Repeat behind.

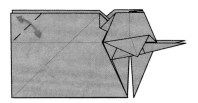

22 Fold and unfold the left side corner to the crease along the middle of the body.

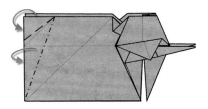

23 Fold the rear edge behind and reverse the fold made in the previous step.

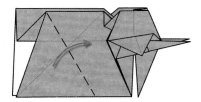

24 Fold the lower left side corner up to the head.

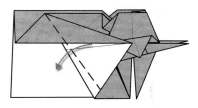

25 Fold the corner back down again. The outer edge should be perpendicular to the top edge.

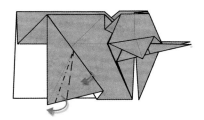

26 Fold the paper into the model, then repeat steps 25 to 26 behind.

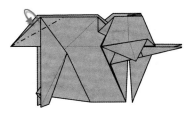

27 Carefully fold the edges of the tail inside the model.

Elephant continued

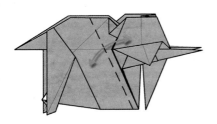

28 Crease fold the whole model, the fold should be parallel to the edge of the folds in the front leg.

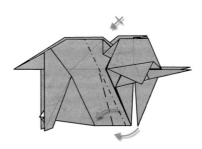

29 Fold the body to bring the front and back together. This will give some shape to the elephant's body.

30 Fold the lower edge up and into the model. Repeat behind.

31 Fold the edges under the legs to narrow them. Note the step shows the layer of paper underneath being folded. Repeat behind.

32 Crimp fold the trunk and reverse fold the tail. Then, fold up a small part of the back leg and repeat behind.

33 Fold the trunk up and the tail down. Then curve the tusks.

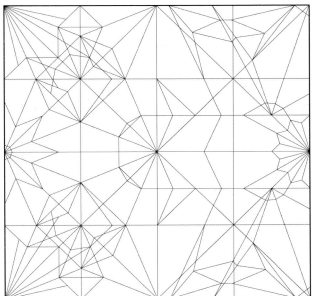

Elephant - advanced

If we unfold the elephant we would have a square of paper with the folded creases marked on the paper. This is the crease pattern for the elephant. It also shows where parts of the paper would end up in the final design. Experienced folders can use crease patterns to fold origami models and some design techniques have evolved to map out a crease pattern as part of the design process.

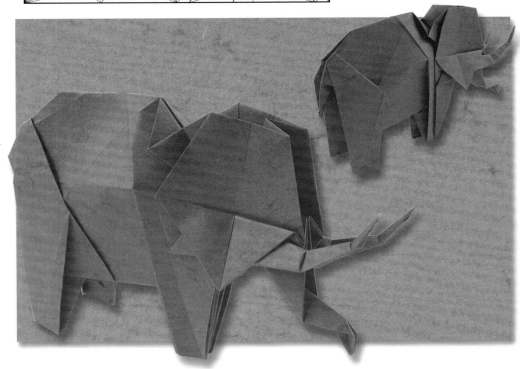

Gallery

Crab

The colour and texture of the paper used to make this large golden crab add character and help to create the illusion of it being alive.

Gorillas

LEFT With a broad, intimidating body and a strong, confident scowl on his face, this gorilla is not one to be messed with. The ability to capture the essence of an object or animal is one of the beauties of origami.

BELOW Gorilla place settings for a dinner at the Natural History Museum.

Fishscape

A beautiful underwater scene made almost entirely from folded paper, teeming with an array of sizes of colourful fish, lobsters, crabs, prawns and seahorses.

Moving stationery

Produced for the opening of a stationery shop, this display shows how effective the use of colour and shape can be in creating a sense of movement.

Index